Is It an Insect?

By Catherine Ripley

ROLLINS ELEMENTARY SCHOOL READING FIRST

CELEBRATION PRESS
Pearson Learning Group

ants

ladybugs

butterfly

grasshopper

There are many kinds of **insects**.

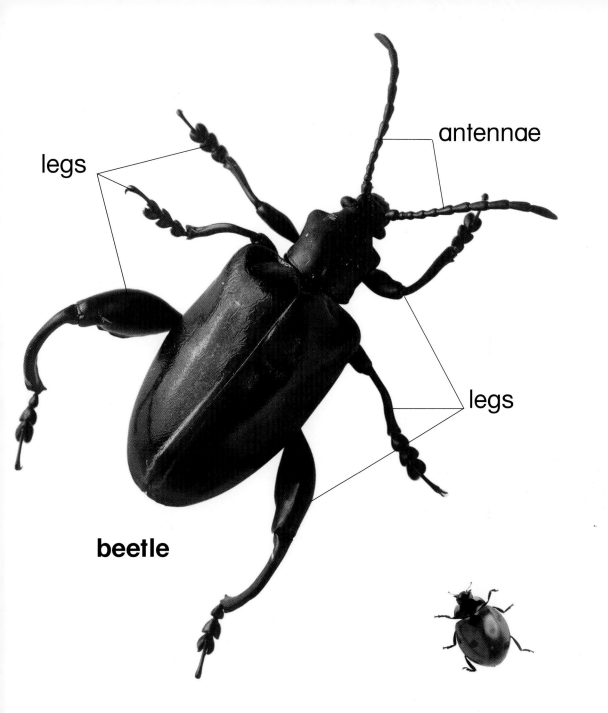

legs

antennae

legs

beetle

All insects have 6 legs.

hornet

thorax

head

abdomen

All insects have 3 body parts.

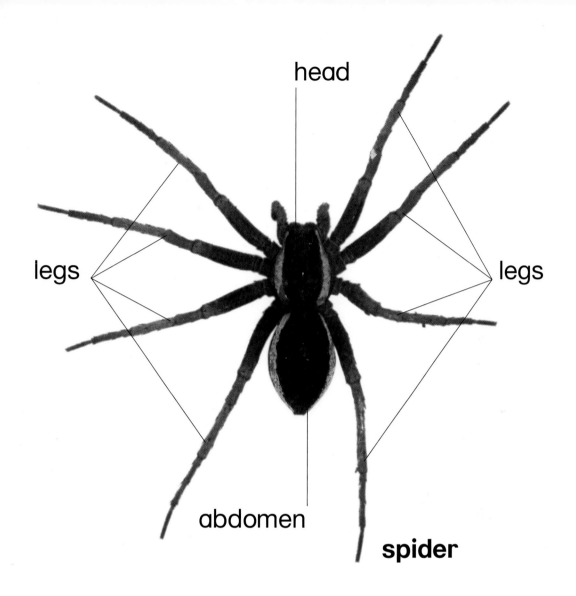

head

legs

legs

abdomen

spider

Spiders have 8 legs
and 2 body parts.

Are spiders insects? No!

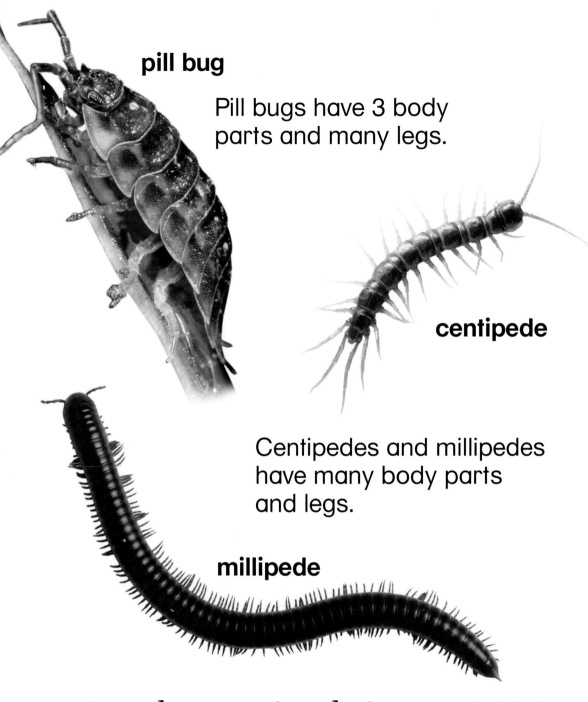

pill bug

Pill bugs have 3 body parts and many legs.

centipede

Centipedes and millipedes have many body parts and legs.

millipede

Are these animals insects? No!

Animal	Number of Legs and Body Parts	Is It an Insect?
ladybug	6 legs 3 body parts	yes
mite	8 legs 2 body parts	no
daddy long legs	8 legs 1 body part	no
ant	6 legs 3 body parts	yes

Is it an insect? Count to be sure.

Glossary

 **abdomen**   the third body part of an insect

 **head**   the first body part of an insect; has two antennae

 **insects**   animals with 6 legs and 3 body parts

 **thorax**   the middle body part of an insect